Especially for
CHRISTIANS

Especially for
CHRISTIANS

✦

Powerful Thought-Provoking Words
from the Past

Mark Alton Rose

iUniverse, Inc.
New York Lincoln Shanghai

Especially for CHRISTIANS
Powerful Thought-Provoking Words from the Past

iUniverse books may be ordered through booksellers or by contacting:

iUniverse
2021 Pine Lake Road, Suite 100
Lincoln, NE 68512
www.iuniverse.com
1-800-Authors (1-800-288-4677)

ISBN-13: 978-0-595-35830-4 (pbk)
ISBN-13: 978-0-595-80293-7 (ebk)
ISBN-10: 0-595-35830-6 (pbk)
ISBN-10: 0-595-80293-1 (ebk)

Printed in the United States of America

You must accept the truth from whatever source it comes.

—*Maimonides (1135–1204)*

The wisdom of the wise and the experience of the ages, may be preserved through quotations.

—*Benjamin Disraeli (1804–1881)*

Acknowledgements

Special thanks to all of the people in this book, past and present. May your words continue to resonate for as long as humanity needs to hear them. Thanks to the memory of my father, John Earl Rose, whose presence was felt greatly in this book-creating process. Thank you for my life, Dad. And very special thanks to Lisa for continuing to believe in me, and for not seeing this book as the ravings of a madman.

Introduction

Truth has a strange way of smacking you in the face when you least expect it. You know, like when you're driving down the road and all of a sudden...BAM! A burst of inspiration. And then you find it difficult to describe the *source* of that inspiration. Truth can be found while reading a good book, seeing a great movie, watching a colorful sunset...or in the breathtaking beauty of the Grand Canyon. Truth is all around us. And yet we all seem to have our own personal definition. Kind of like spirituality. So, I suppose the ultimate truth is when we finally give in to the realization that we don't know everything. That there are certain things we will *never* know as long as we are inhabiting a physical body.

Before I get into why this book is entitled *Especially for Christians,* let me tell you a little bit about myself. I was born in 1961 in a small town in the Piedmont of North Carolina. I suppose some would call it "The Bible Belt". My father was raised as a Methodist and my mother a Baptist. My brother and I were fortunate in that our parents never forced any religion on us...never made us go to church (unless we wanted to).

Dad was a teacher and a wanderer, so we moved around quite a bit when I was a child. We moved to Colorado then to Arizona then to Nevada...then back to North Carolina...then back to Nevada...and finally, after I graduated from high school, back to North Carolina. When you do that much traveling, you get to experience a lot of things and a lot of different cultures. At one point we lived on an Indian reservation where dad was teaching. Yes, I have had the opportunity to experience a great many things...thanks to my father's wandering spirit.

When I was 18, a high school buddy and I took a few months off to go ride bicycles in England and Scotland. I was in awe of all the magnificent cathedrals and castles...and the amazing history of the place. I thought about how much beautiful architecture had been constructed in the name of God. I also thought about all of the people who had been killed in His holy name. As far as I can remember, that trip was the real beginning of my questioning nature. I returned to the United States to discover that my parents were getting a divorce. Then the questions really began.

Fast forward to 1987. After graduating from college with my degree in theatre arts, I quickly got a job at a small gospel radio station. I had to do a lot of weekend work, and that was when most of the country preachers came in to do their live broadcasts. Many of them would preach about how God is a *vengeful, jealous* god…but he *loves* you. Somehow I didn't find a lot of comfort (or logic) in that. A *loving* god with qualities that man despises in himself?

The following year I decided to pursue my acting career and moved to New York City with a few friends. It was there that my spiritual struggle took a different turn. And seeing all of the homeless people living in the streets of the city wasn't helping matters. One day when I was feeling a bit depressed (as was often the case in New York), I was channel surfing and came upon *The 700 Club*. The program seemed to have what I was looking for, and after that day I began to watch it "religiously". Pat Robertson had a way of intellectualizing Christianity in a way that was very appealing. I now had something in common with thousands (millions?) of other people…I had become mesmerized by a charismatic television evangelist. I wanted more. I needed more. I was willing to do anything God asked of me. Then, one day Mr. Robertson was talking about a new movie that was about to be released entitled *The Last Temptation of Christ*. He was imploring his viewers to write letters to the movie studio, and to please ask the producers not to release the film. It was his belief that it would show Jesus in a negative light. Well, needless to say, I was one of the people who wrote letters that day. I sat down and typed out a long three page epistle explaining why they should not release this movie to the public. Keep in mind, I knew nothing about the film, or the book on which it was based. I was simply doing what the man on the television told me to do.

Later that year I moved from New York to Virginia Beach, Virginia, thinking I might get work as an actor at Pat Robertson's organization. I ended up working at a Contemporary Christian radio station (that he owned). *The Last Temptation of Christ* was soon released to movie theaters amid controversy. I thought back to my part in it. By writing that letter, had I done what *God* wanted me to do? Or had I just been listening to a *man* with an *opinion?* I decided to cross the picket lines and see the movie for myself. As it turned out, it was one of the most beautiful movies I had ever seen. A "what if" tale about Jesus. I had *pre-judged* the film without reason. I suppose you could say that was when I had my "spiritual awakening". Should I continue listening to the opinions of mortal men on a television screen, or should I take charge of my own spirituality and begin thinking for myself? I chose the latter…and I never looked back.

Losing my father to Alzheimer's Disease this past year has given me a unique perspective on life. I was with him during his last moments on earth as a physical being. As I looked into his eyes at that final second, it seemed as though I could actually sense his spirit leaving his body. It was an amazing experience. And I somehow knew he was going to be alright. My father was never what you would call a deeply religious man, but he always knew that life was a continuing process, and that death was nothing more than a continuation of life in another form.

This book is entitled *Especially for Christians* basically because Christianity is the religion I have been exposed to all my life. It could easily have been called *Especially for Muslims* or *Especially for Hindus* or *Especially for Jews* or…whatever. I gave it that title because of my concern about the role of religion, in general, on this planet. I know all too well how easy it is to become "fanatical" in a chosen religion.

I always thought the true meaning of the word "Christian" was "one who puts into action the words of Jesus of Nazareth." As one who greatly respects the *pure* teachings of this great philosopher, I sometimes find it amusing the many ways in which *religion* attempts to put its own spin on his words. Actually, the Judeo Christian Bible has been translated and re-translated so many times over the centuries that we don't really know exactly what he said. But when you look at the basics, it was just plain common sense. I really think to be a true Christian requires one to have and keep an open mind…and not to lose oneself in the symbolism and emotional nature of *religion.*

This book is a compilation of thoughts taken from some of the great minds of humanity's past and present. There are no chapters, only the words themselves, and a brief glossary of the sources at the end. Before you begin reading these words it is very important for you to realize that this book is not anti-religion. That was never my intent. It is more of a call to individuals to take more personal responsibility for their own spirituality…their own *truth.* And perhaps be less of a follower. That being said, I hope you will approach the following pages with an open mind. And remember, truth is all around you. You simply need to be open to it.

Mark Alton Rose
February 9, 2005
Hickory, North Carolina

I believe in an America where the separation of church and state is absolute—where no Catholic prelate would tell the President (should he be Catholic) how to act, and no Protestant minister would tell his parishioners for whom to vote—where no church or church school is granted any public funds or political preference—and where no man is denied public office merely because his religion differs from the President who might appoint him or the people who might elect him. I believe in an America that is officially neither Catholic, Protestant nor Jewish—where no public official either requests or accepts instructions on public policy from the Pope, the National Council of Churches or any other ecclesiastical source—where no religious body seeks to impose its will directly or indirectly upon the general populace or the public acts of its officials—and where religious liberty is so indivisible that an act against one church is treated as an act against all.

—*John F. Kennedy (1917–1963)*

✦

The question before the human race is, whether the God of nature shall govern the world by his own laws, or whether priests and kings shall rule it by fictitious miracles?

—*John Adams (1735–1826)*

✦

I am the wisest man alive, for I know one thing, and that is that I know nothing.

—*Socrates (470 BC–399 BC)*

There are more things in heaven and earth, Horatio, than are dreamt
of in your philosophy.

—William Shakespeare (1564–1616)
From "Hamlet"

✦

If a man should conquer in battle a thousand, and a thousand more,
and another should conquer himself, his would be the greater victory,
because the greatest of victories is the victory over oneself.

—Siddhartha Gautama (563–483 BC)

✦

What lies behind us and what lies before us are small matters compared
to what lies within us.

—Ralph Waldo Emerson (1803–1882)

✦

You can't convince a believer of anything; for their belief is not based
on evidence, it's based on a deep seated need to believe.

—Dr. Carl Sagan (1934–1996)

Don't judge each day by the harvest you reap, but by the seeds you plant.

—*Robert Louis Stevenson (1850–1894)*

◆

If God did not exist, it would be necessary to invent Him.

—*Voltaire (1694–1778)*

◆

Man is the religious animal. He is the only religious animal. He is the only animal that has the True Religion…*several* of them. He is the only animal that loves his neighbor as himself and cuts his throat, if his theology isn't straight. He has made a graveyard of the globe in trying his honest best to smooth his brother's path to happiness and heaven.

—*Mark Twain (1835–1910)*

◆

I would rather have a mind opened by wonder than one closed by belief.

—*Gerry Spence (1929–)*

I never cease being dumbfounded by the unbelievable things people believe.

—Leo Rosten (1908–1997)

✦

I almost shudder at the thought of alluding to the most fatal example of the abuses of grief which the history of mankind has preserved…the Cross. Consider what calamities that engine of grief has produced.

—John Adams (1735–1826)

✦

The state of your life is nothing more than a reflection of your state of mind.

—Dr. Wayne W. Dyer (1940–)

✦

I am convinced that human nature is basically gentle, not aggressive. And every one of us has a responsibility to act as if all our thoughts, words, and deeds matter. For, really, they do.

—Dalai Lama (1935–)

If we could see ourselves and other objects as they really are, we should see ourselves in a world of spiritual natures, our community with which neither began at our birth nor will end with the death of the body.

—Immanuel Kant (1724–1804)

✦

I cannot believe for a moment that life in the first instance originated on this insignificant little ball which we call the earth…The particles which combined to evolve living creatures on this planet of ours probably came from some other body elsewhere in the universe.

—Thomas Edison (1847–1931)

✦

Imagine there's no countries…It isn't hard to do…Nothing to kill or die for…And no religion too…Imagine all the people living life in peace…

—John Lennon (1940–1980)

✦

The authors of the gospels were unlettered and ignorant men and the teachings of Jesus have come to us mutilated, misstated and unintelligible.

—Thomas Jefferson (1762–1826)

There are only two ways to live your life. One is as though nothing is a miracle. The other is as though everything is a miracle.

—Albert Einstein (1879–1955)

✦

Do not believe in anything simply because you have heard it. Do not believe in anything simply because it is spoken and rumored by many. Do not believe in anything simply because it is found written in your religious books. Do not believe in anything merely on the authority of your teachers and elders. Do not believe in traditions because they have been handed down for many generations. But after observation and analysis, when you find that anything agrees with reason and is conducive to the good and benefit of one and all, then accept it and live up to it.

—Siddhartha Gautama (563–483 BC)

✦

You have to leave the city of your comfort and go into the wilderness of your intuition. What you'll discover will be wonderful. What you'll discover is yourself.

—Alan Alda (1936–)

✦

I went to the woods because I wanted to live deliberately, I wanted to live deep and suck out all the marrow of life, To put to rout all that was not life and not when I had come to die discover that I had not lived.

—Henry David Thoreau (1817–1862)

Every national church or religion has established itself by pretending some special mission from God…as if the way to God was not open to every man alike.

—*Thomas Paine (1737–1809)*

✦

I do not consider it an insult, but rather a compliment to be called an agnostic. I do not pretend to *know,* where many ignorant men are *sure*…that is all that agnosticism means.

—*Clarence Darrow (1857–1938)*

✦

Men have ascribed to God imperfections that they would deplore in themselves.

—*W. Somerset Maugham (1874–1965)*

✦

What influence, in fact, have ecclesiastical establishments had on society? In some instances they have been seen to erect a spiritual tyranny on the ruins of the civil authority; in many instances they have been seen upholding the thrones of political tyranny; in no instance have they been the guardians of the liberties of the people. Rulers who wish to subvert the public liberty may have found an established clergy convenient allies. A just government, instituted to secure and perpetuate it, needs them not.

—*James Madison (1751–1836)*

It is a truism that almost any sect, cult, or religion will legislate its creed into law if it acquires the political power to do so, and will follow it by suppressing opposition, subverting all education to seize early the minds of the young, and by killing, locking up, or driving underground all heretics.

—Robert Heinlein (1907–1988)

✦

I would never die for my beliefs because I might be wrong.

—Bertrand Russell (1872–1970)

✦

Shake off all the fears of servile prejudices, under which weak minds are servilely crouched. Fix reason firmly in her seat, and call on her tribunal for every fact, every opinion. Question with boldness even the existence of a God; because, if there be one, he must more approve of the homage of reason than that of blindfolded fear.

—Thomas Jefferson (1762–1826)

✦

I do not feel obliged to believe that the same God who has endowed us with sense, reason, and intellect has intended us to forgo their use.

—Galileo Galilei (1564–1642)

People fashion their God after their own understanding. They make their God first and worship him afterwards.

—*Oscar Wilde (1854–1900)*

✦

My religion consists of a humble admiration of the illimitable superior spirit who reveals himself in the slight details we are able to perceive with our frail and feeble minds. That deeply emotional conviction of the presence of a superior reasoning power, which is revealed in the incomprehensible universe, forms my idea of God.

—*Albert Einstein (1879–1955)*

✦

The Bible contains legendary, historical and ethical contents. It is quite possible to consider them separately, and one doesn't have to accept the legends in order to get the ethics. Fundamentalists make a grave mistake to insist on the letter of the writings, because they drive away many who can't swallow the Adam-and-Eve bit.

—*Isaac Asimov (1920–1992)*

The priesthood have, in all ancient nations, nearly monopolized learning. And even since the Reformation, when or where has existed a Protestant or dissenting sect who would tolerate A FREE INQUIRY? The blackest billingsgate, the most ungentlemanly insolence, the most yahooish brutality, is patently endured, countenanced, propagated, and applauded. But touch a solemn truth in collision with the dogma of a sect, though capable of the clearest proof, and you will soon find you have disturbed a nest, and the hornets will swarm about your legs and hands, and fly into your face and eyes.

—John Adams (1735–1826)

✦

If you have two religions in your land, the two will cut each other's throats; but if you have thirty religions, they will dwell in peace.

—Voltaire (1694–1778)

✦

Those who invalidate reason ought seriously to consider whether they argue against reason with or without reason; if with reason, then they establish the principles that they are laboring to dethrone: but if they argue without reason (which, in order to be consistent with themselves they must do), they are out of reach of rational conviction, nor do they deserve a rational argument.

—Ethan Allen (1738–1789)

It is a fine thing to establish one's own religion in one's heart, not to be dependent on tradition and second-hand ideals. Life will seem to you, later, not a lesser, but a greater thing.

—D.H. Lawrence (1885–1930)

✦

When a true genius appears in the world, you may know him by this sign, that the dunces are all in confederacy against him.

—Jonathan Swift (1667–1745)

✦

Whatever affects one directly, affects all indirectly. I can never be what I ought to be until you are what you ought to be. This is the interrelated structure of reality.

—Martin Luther King, Jr. (1929–1968)

✦

I believe in the brotherhood of man and the uniqueness of the individual. But if you ask me to prove what I believe, I can't. You know them to be true but you could spend a whole lifetime without being able to prove them. The mind can proceed only so far upon what it knows and can prove. There comes a point where the mind takes a higher plane of knowledge, but can never prove how it got there. All great discoveries have involved such a leap.

—Albert Einstein (1879–1955)

Religions are many and diverse, but reason and goodness are one.

—Elbert Hubbard (1856–1915)

✦

From what may anyone be saved? Only from themselves! That is, their individual hell. They dig it with their own desires.

—Edgar Cayce (1877–1945)

✦

My earlier views of the unsoundness of the Christian scheme of salvation and the human origin of the scriptures, have become clearer and stronger with advancing years and I see no reason for thinking I shall ever change them.

—Abraham Lincoln (1809–1865)

✦

If 50 million people believe a foolish thing, it is still a foolish thing.

—Anatole France (1844–1924)

Thus all things altered. Nothing dies. And here and there the unbodied spirit flies.

—*Ovid (43 BC–17 AD)*

✦

In every country and every age, the priest has been hostile to liberty. He is always in alliance with the despot…they have perverted the purest religion ever preached to man into mystery and jargon, unintelligible to all mankind, and therefore the safer engine for their purpose.

—*Thomas Jefferson (1762–1826)*

✦

This is what you shall do: Love the earth and sun and animals, despise riches, give alms to everyone that asks, stand up for the stupid and crazy, devote your income and labor to others, hate tyrants, argue not concerning God.

—*Walt Whitman (1819–1892)*

✦

Believe nothing, no matter where you read it, or who said it, no matter if I have said it, unless it agrees with your own reason and your own common sense.

—*Siddhartha Gautama (563–483 BC)*

The Christian religion, then, is not an affair of preaching, or prating, or ranting, but of taking care of the bodies as well as the souls of people; not an affair of belief and of faith and of professions, but an affair of doing good, and especially to those who are in want; not an affair of fire and brimstone, but an affair of bacon and bread, beer and a bed.

—William Cobbett (1763–1835)

✦

Leave the matter of religion to the family altar, the church, and the private school, supported entirely by private contributions. Keep the church and state forever separate.

—Ulysses S. Grant (1822–1885)

✦

It is one of our perennial problems, whether there is actually a God. From the Hindu point of view each soul is divine. All religions are branches of one big tree. It doesn't matter what you call Him just as long as you call. Just as cinematic images appear to be real but are only combinations of light and shade, so is the universal variety a delusion. The planetary spheres, with their countless forms of life, are naught but figures in a cosmic motion picture. One's values are profoundly changed when he is finally convinced that creation is only a vast motion picture and that not in, but beyond, lies his own ultimate reality.

—George Harrison (1943–2001)

I can imagine no greater misfortune for a cultured people than to see in the hands of the rulers not only the civil, but also the religious power.

—*Catullus (84 BC–54 BC)*

✦

Of all religions the Christian is without doubt the one which should inspire tolerance most, although, up to now the Christians have been the most intolerant of all men.

—*Voltaire (1694–1778)*

✦

All major religious traditions carry basically the same message, that is love, compassion and forgiveness…the important thing is they should be part of our daily lives.

—*Dalai Lama (1935–)*

✦

Science may have found a cure for most evils, but it has found no remedy for the worst of them all…the apathy of human beings.

—*Helen Keller (1880–1968)*

If something comes to life in others because of you, then you have
made an approach to immortality.

—*Norman Cousins (1912–1990)*

✦

A tyrant must put on the appearance of uncommon devotion to
religion. Subjects are less apprehensive of illegal treatment from a ruler
whom they consider god-fearing and pious. On the other hand, they
do less easily move against him, believing that he has the gods on his
side.

—*Aristotle (384 BC–322 BC)*

✦

We all remember how many religious wars were fought for a religion of
love and gentleness; how many bodies were burned alive with the
genuinely kind intention of saving souls from the eternal fire of hell.

—*Karl Popper (1902–1994)*

✦

The church is always trying to get other people to reform; it might not
be a bad idea to reform itself a little, by way of example.

—*Mark Twain (1835–1910)*

In the long term we can hope that religion will change the nature of man and reduce conflict. But history is not encouraging in this respect. The bloodiest wars in history have been religious wars.

—*Richard M. Nixon (1913–1994)*

✦

Religion is not a fractional thing that can be doled out in fixed weekly or daily measures as one among various subjects in the school syllabus. It is the truth of our complete being, the consciousness of our personal relationship with the infinite.

—*Rabindranath Tagore (1861–1941)*

✦

And who can doubt that it will lead to the worst disorders when minds created free by God are compelled to submit slavishly to an outside will? When we are told to deny our senses and subject them to the whim of others? When people devoid of whatsoever competence are made judges over experts and are granted authority to treat them as they please? These are the novelties which are apt to bring about the ruin of commonwealths and the subversion of the state.

—*Galileo Galilei (1564–1642)*

✦

The introduction of religious passion into politics is the end of honest politics, and the introduction of politics into religion is the prostitution of true religion.

—*Lord Hailsham (1872–1950)*

What havoc has been made of books through every century of the Christian era? Where are fifty gospels, condemned as spurious by the bull of Pope Gelasius? Where are the forty wagon-loads of Hebrew manuscripts burned in France, by order of another pope, because of suspected heresy? Remember the 'index expurgatorius', the inquisition, the stake, the axe, the halter and the guillotine; and, oh! horrible, the rack! This is as bad, if not worse, than a slow fire. Nor should the Lion's Mouth be forgotten. Have you considered that system of holy lies and pious frauds that has raged and triumphed for 1,500 years.

—*John Adams (1735–1826)*

◆

Every religion is true one way or another. It is true when understood metaphorically. But when it gets stuck in its own metaphors, interpreting them as facts, then you are in trouble.

—*Joseph Campbell (1904–1987)*

◆

The body of Benjamin Franklin, Printer, like the cover of an old book, its contents torn out and stripped of its lettering and gilding, lies here…Yet the Work itself shall not be lost; for it will, as he believed, appear once more in a new and more beautiful edition, corrected and amended by the Author.

—*Epitaph of Benjamin Franklin (1706–1790)*

There is no religion without love, and people may talk as much as they like about their religion, but if it does not teach them to be good and kind to man and beast, it is all a sham.

—Anna Sewell (1820–1878)

✦

Say nothing of my religion. It is known to God and myself alone. Its evidence before the world is to be sought in my life: if it has been honest and dutiful to society the religion which has regulated it cannot be a bad one.

—Thomas Jefferson (1762–1826)

✦

I always distrust people who know so much about what God wants them to do to their fellows.

—Susan B. Anthony (1820–1906)

✦

Learn to get in touch with the silence within yourself and know that everything in life has a purpose.

—Elisabeth Kübler-Ross (1926–2004)

What befalls the earth befalls all the sons of the earth. This we know: the earth does not belong to man, man belongs to the earth. All things are connected like the blood that unites us all. Man does not weave this web of life. He is merely a strand of it. Whatever he does to the web, he does to himself.

—*Chief Seattle (1786–1866)*

✦

In the matter of religion, people eagerly fasten their eyes on the difference between their own creed and yours; whilst the charm of the study is in finding the agreements and identities in all the religions of humanity.

—*Ralph Waldo Emerson (1803–1882)*

✦

Men exist for the sake of one another.

—*Marcus Aurelius (121 AD–180 AD)*

✦

Our birth is but a sleep and a forgetting; The soul that rises with us, our life's star, hath had elsewhere its setting, and cometh from afar; Not in entire forgetfulness, and not in utter nakedness, but railing clouds of glory do we come from God, who is our home.

—*William Wordsworth (1770–1850)*

I could not, at any age, be content to take my place by the fireside and simply look on. Life was meant to be lived. Curiosity must be kept alive. One must never, for whatever reason, turn his back on life.

—Eleanor Roosevelt (1884–1962)

✦

Whether one believes in a religion or not, and whether one believes in rebirth or not, there isn't anyone who doesn't appreciate kindness and compassion.

—Dalai Lama (1935–)

✦

For what is Mysticism? Is it not the attempt to draw near to God, not by rites or ceremonies, but by inward disposition? Is it not merely a hard word for 'The Kingdom of Heaven is within'? Heaven is neither a place nor a time.

—Florence Nightingale (1820–1910)

✦

Experience witnesseth that ecclesiastical establishments, instead of maintaining the purity and efficacy of religion, have had a contrary operation. During almost fifteen centuries has the legal establishment of Christianity been on trial. What has been its fruits? More or less, in all places, pride and indolence in the clergy; ignorance and servility in the laity; in both, superstition, bigotry and persecution.

—James Madison (1751–1836)

Meditation is not a means to an end. It is both the means and the end.

—*Jiddu Krishnamurti (1895–1986)*

✦

The best and most beautiful things in the world cannot be seen, nor touched…but are felt in the heart.

—*Helen Keller (1880–1968)*

✦

If we are to respect others' religions as we would have them to respect our own, a friendly study of the world's religion is a sacred duty.

—*Mahatma Gandhi (1869–1948)*

✦

One who is injured ought not to return the injury, for on no account can it be right to do an injustice; and it is not right to return an injury, or to do evil to any man, however much we have suffered from him.

—*Socrates (470 BC–399 BC)*

To believe in God or in a guiding force because someone tells you to is the height of stupidity. We are given senses to receive our information within. With our own eyes we see, and with our own skin we feel. With our intelligence, it is intended that we understand. But each person must puzzle it out for himself or herself.

—Sophy Burnham (1936–)

✦

To believe in God for me is to feel that there is a God, not a dead one, or a stuffed one, but a living one, who with irresistible force urges us towards more loving.

—Vincent van Gogh (1853–1890)

✦

He who sows the ground with care and diligence acquires a greater stock of religious merit than he could gain by the repetition of ten thousand prayers.

—Zoroaster (628 BC–551 BC)

✦

Religion is regarded by the common people as true, by the wise as false, and by the rulers as useful.

—Seneca (3 BC–65 AD)

Change your thoughts and you change your world.

—*Norman Vincent Peale (1898–1993)*

✦

Convince a man that he is an animal, that his own dignity and self-respect are delusions, that there is no 'beyond' to aspire to, no higher potential self to achieve, and you have a slave. Let a man know he is himself, a spiritual being, that he is capable of the power of choice and has the right to aspire to greater wisdom, and you have started him up a higher road.

—*L. Ron Hubbard (1911–1986)*

✦

This is my simple religion. There is no need for temples; no need for complicated philosophy. Our own brain, our own heart is our temple; the philosophy is kindness.

—*Dalai Lama (1935–)*

✦

Everyone ought to worship God according to his own inclinations, and not to be constrained by force.

—*Flavius Josephus (37 AD–100 AD)*

Fear is the path to the dark side. Fear leads to anger. Anger leads to
hate. Hate leads to suffering.

—Yoda

✦

Truth is the beginning of every good thing, both in heaven and on
earth; and he who would be blessed and happy should be from the first
a partaker of truth, for then he can be trusted.

—Plato (428 BC–348 BC)

✦

All national institutions of churches, whether Jewish, Christian, or
Turkish, appear to me no other than human inventions, set up to
terrify and enslave mankind, and monopolize power and profit.

—Thomas Paine (1737–1809)

✦

Smiling is very important. If we are not able to smile, then the world
will not have peace. It is not by going out for a demonstration against
nuclear missiles that we can bring about peace. It is with our capacity
of smiling, breathing, and being peace that we can make peace.

—Thich Nhat Hanh (1926–)

You give but little when you give of your possessions. It is when you give of yourself that you truly give.

—*Kahlil Gibran (1883–1931)*

✦

All the kindness which a man puts out into the world works on the heart and thoughts of mankind.

—*Albert Schweitzer (1875–1965)*

✦

Dwelling on the negative simply contributes to its power.

—*Shirley MacLaine (1934–)*

✦

Yesterday is but a dream, tomorrow but a vision. But today well lived makes every yesterday a dream of happiness, and every tomorrow a vision of hope. Look well, therefore, to this day.

—*Sanskrit Proverb*

Only a life lived for others is a life worth living!

—*Albert Einstein (1879–1955)*

✦

Be master of mind rather than mastered by mind.

—*Zen Proverb*

✦

Of all the animosities which have existed among mankind, those which are caused by difference of sentiments in religion appear to be the most inveterate and distressing, and ought to be deprecated. I was in hopes that the enlightened and liberal policy, which has marked the present age, would at least have reconciled Christians of every denomination so far that we should never again see the religious disputes carried to such a pitch as to endanger the peace of society.

—*George Washington (1732–1799)*

✦

In the midst of movement and chaos, keep stillness inside of you.

—*Deepak Chopra (1947–)*

Don't join the book burners. Do not think you are going to conceal thoughts by concealing evidence that they ever existed.

—Dwight D. Eisenhower (1890–1969)

✦

Opportunity, not obligation, is the cornerstone of religion, the basis of all spirituality. So long as you see it the other way around, you will have missed the point.

—Neale Donald Walsch (1943–)
From "Conversations With God (Book I)"

✦

Generally speaking, the errors in religion are dangerous; those in philosophy only ridiculous.

—David Hume (1711–1776)

✦

There seems to be a law that governs all our actions, so I never make plans.

—Greta Garbo (1905–1990)

When one door of happiness closes, another opens; but often we look so long at the closed door that we do not see the one which has been opened for us.

—Helen Keller (1880–1968)

✦

All religions are founded on the fear of the many and the cleverness of the few.

—Stendhal (1783–1842)

✦

We are not human beings having a spiritual experience. We are spiritual beings having a human experience.

—Pierre Teilhard de Chardin (1881–1955)

✦

If someone had told me I would be Pope one day, I would have studied harder.

—Pope John Paul I (1912–1978)

When the missionaries came to Africa they had the Bible and we had the land. They said "Let us pray." We closed our eyes. When we opened them we had the Bible and they had the land.

—Bishop Desmond Tutu (1931–)

✦

More people have been slaughtered in the name of religion than for any other single reason. That, my friends, that is true perversion.

—Harvey Milk (1930–1978)

✦

I like the silent church before the service begins, better than any preaching.

—Ralph Waldo Emerson (1803–1882)

✦

It is possible that mankind is on the threshold of a golden age; but, if so, it will be necessary first to slay the dragon that guards the door, and this dragon is religion.

—Bertrand Russell (1872–1970)

Rarely do we find men who willingly engage in hard, solid thinking. There is an almost universal quest for easy answers and half-baked solutions. Nothing pains some people more than having to think.

—Martin Luther King Jr. (1929–1968)

✦

I do not believe that any type of religion should ever be introduced into the public schools of the United States.

—Thomas Edison (1847–1931)

✦

Those things that nature denied to human sight, she revealed to the eyes of the soul.

—Ovid (43 BC–17 AD)

✦

If the freedom of religion, guaranteed to us by law in theory, can ever rise in practice under the overbearing inquisition of public opinion, then and only then will truth, prevail over fanaticism.

—Thomas Jefferson (1762–1826)

Nature is an unlimited broadcasting station, through which God
speaks to us every hour, if we only will tune in.

—George Washington Carver (1864–1943)

✦

Theology is the box of Pandora; and if it is impossible to shut it, it is at
least useful to inform men, that this fatal box is open.

—Henry Bolingbroke (1678-1751)

✦

Whenever philosophy has taken into its plan religion, it has ended in
skepticism; and whenever religion excludes philosophy, or the spirit of
free inquiry, it leads to willful blindness and superstition.

—Samuel Taylor Coleridge (1772–1834)

✦

General tradition, or the unanimous consent of mankind, is no
criterion of truth.

—Pierre Bayle (1647–1706)

The measure of a mind's evolution is its acceptance of the unacceptable.

—Thea Alexander (1936–)
From the novel "2150 AD"

✦

A Cherokee elder sitting with his grandchildren told them, "In every life there is a terrible fight. A fight between two wolves. One is evil: he is fear, anger, envy, greed, arrogance, self-pity, resentment, and deceit. The other is good: joy, serenity, humility, confidence, generosity, truth, gentleness, and compassion." A child asked, "Grandfather, which wolf will win?" The elder looked him in the eye, "The one you feed."

—Author Unknown

✦

The greatest tragedy in mankind's entire history may be the hijacking of morality by religion.

—Arthur C. Clarke (1917–)

✦

As I understand the Christian religion, it was, and is, a revelation. But how has it happened that millions of fables, tales, legends, have been blended with both Jewish and Christian revelation that have made them the most bloody religion that ever existed?

—John Adams (1735–1826)

Government is an evil; it is only the thoughtlessness and vices of men that make it a necessary evil. When all men are good and wise, government will of itself decay.

—Percy Bysshe Shelley (1792–1822)

✦

When we blindly adopt a religion, a political system, a literary dogma, we become automatons. We cease to grow.

—Anais Nin (1903–1977)

✦

Of late, instead of saying God is Truth I have been saying Truth is God, in order more fully to define my religion. I used at one time to know by heart the thousand names of God which a booklet in Hinduism gives in verse form and which perhaps tens of thousands recite every morning. But nowadays nothing so completely describes my God as Truth. Denial of God we have known. Denial of Truth we have not known. The most ignorant among mankind have some truth in them. We are all sparks of Truth. The sum total of these sparks is indescribable, as-yet-Unknown Truth, which is God. I am being daily led nearer to it by constant prayer. The bearing of this religion on social life is, or has to be, seen in one's daily social contact. To be true to such religion one has to lose oneself in continuous and continuing service of all life. Realization of Truth is impossible without a complete merging of oneself in and identification with this limitless ocean of life. Hence, for me, there is no escape from social service; there is no happiness on earth beyond or apart from it. Social service here must be taken to include every department of life. In this scheme there is nothing low, nothing high. For all is one, though we seem to be many.

—Mahatma Gandhi (1869–1948)

Men never do evil so completely and cheerfully as when they do it from religious conviction.

—Blaise Pascal (1623–1662)

✦

The light of men is justice. Quench it not with the contrary winds of oppression and tyranny. The purpose of justice is the appearance of unity among men.

—Mirza Hoseyn Ali Nuri (1817-1892)

✦

As you press on for justice, be sure to move with dignity and discipline, using only the weapon of love. Let no man pull you so low as to hate him. Always avoid violence. If you succumb to the temptation of using violence in your struggle, unborn generations will be the recipients of a long and desolate night of bitterness, and your chief legacy to the future will be an endless reign of meaningless chaos.

—Martin Luther King Jr. (1929–1968)

✦

Christian Fundamentalism: The doctrine that there is an absolutely powerful, infinitely knowledgeable, universe spanning entity that is deeply and personally concerned about my sex life.

—Andrew Lias

Many honest people should have a more tranquil mind if they were assured that they had only a blind destiny for their guide: they tremble more in thinking that there is a God, than if they believed that he did not exist.

—Lord Anthony Ashley Cooper Shaftesbury III (1671-1713)

✦

There seems to be a terrible misunderstanding on the part of a great many people to the effect that when you cease to believe you may cease to behave.

—Louis Kronenberger (1904–1980)

✦

I cannot conceive otherwise than that He, the Infinite Father, expects or requires no worship or praise from us, but that He is even infinitely above it.

—Benjamin Franklin (1706–1790)

✦

When you make a mistake, don't look back at it long. Take the reason of the thing into your mind, and then look forward. Mistakes are lessons of wisdom. The past cannot be changed. The future is yet in your power.

—Phyllis Bottome (1884–1963)

We all live with the objective of being happy; our lives are all different
and yet the same.

—*Anne Frank (1929–1945)*

✦

In faith and hope the world will disagree, but all mankind's concern is
charity.

—*Alexander the Great (356 BC–323 BC)*

✦

Those who can make you believe absurdities can make you commit
attrocities.

—*Voltaire (1694–1778)*

✦

Every religion is good that teaches man to be good; and I know of none
that instructs him to be bad.

—*Thomas Paine (1737–1809)*

I have just three things to teach: simplicity, patience, compassion.
These three are your greatest treasures.

—Lao-tzu (Born 600 BC)

✦

A pious man is one who would be an atheist if the king were.

—Jean de la Bruyère (1645–1696)

✦

If there is anything we wish to change in a child, we should first see if it
is not something that could better be changed in ourselves.

—Carl Jung (1875–1961)

✦

How many observe Christ's birthday! How few, his precepts! O! 'tis
easier to keep holidays than commandments.

—Benjamin Franklin (1706–1790)

No man ever believes that the Bible means what it says: He is always convinced that it says what he means.

—*George Bernard Shaw (1856–1950)*

✦

If Jesus had been killed twenty years ago, Catholic school children would be wearing little electric chairs around their necks instead of crosses.

—*Lenny Bruce (1925–1966)*

✦

Walk with those seeking Truth. Run from those who think they've found it

—*Deepak Chopra (1947–)*

✦

Every beauty which is seen here below by persons of perception resemble more than anything else that celestial source from which we all are come.

—*Michelangelo (1475–1564)*

The conquering of self is truly greater than were one to conquer many worlds.

—*Edgar Cayce (1877–1945)*

✦

To surrender to ignorance and call it God has always been premature, and it remains premature today.

—*Isaac Asimov (1920–1992)*

✦

To have a positive religion is not necessary. To be in harmony with yourself and the universe is what counts, and this is possible without positive and specific formulation in words.

—*Johann Wolfgang von Goethe (1749–1832)*

✦

Everything that we think God has in his mind necessarily proceeds from our own mind; it is what we imagine to be in God's mind, and it is really difficult for human intelligence to guess at a divine intelligence. What we usually end up with by this sort of reasoning is to make God the color-sergeant of our army and to make Him as chauvinistic as ourselves.

—*Lin Yutang (1895–1976)*

Religions are all alike—founded upon fables and mythologies.

—*Thomas Jefferson (1762–1826)*

✦

With most people unbelief in one thing is founded upon blind belief in
another.

—*Georg Christoph Lichtenberg (1742–1799)*

✦

The further the spiritual evolution of mankind advances, the more
certain it seems to me that the path to genuine religiosity does not lie
through the fear of life, and the fear of death, and blind faith, but
through striving after rational knowledge.

—*Albert Einstein (1879–1955)*

✦

One of the first things to learn if you want to be a contemplative is to
mind your own business. Nothing is more suspicious, in a man who
seems holy, than an impatient desire to reform other men.

—*Thomas Merton (1915–1968)*

Men rarely (if ever) manage to dream up a god superior to themselves. Most gods have the manners and morals of a spoiled child.

—*Robert Heinlein (1907–1988)*

✦

It's all make believe, isn't it?

—*Marilyn Monroe (1926–1962)*

✦

I wish it (Christianity) were more productive of good works…I mean real good works…not holy-day keeping, sermon-hearing…or making long prayers, filled with flatteries and compliments despised by wise men, and much less capable of pleasing the Deity.

—*Benjamin Franklin (1706–1790)*

✦

Be born anywhere, little embryo novelist, but do not be born under the shadow of a great creed, not under the burden of original sin, not under the doom of salvation. Go out and be born among the gypsies or thieves or among happy workaday people who live in the sun and do not think about their souls.

—*Pearl S. Buck (1892–1973)*

Choose only one master…Nature.

—*Rembrandt (1606–1669)*

✦

Truth is so great a perfection, that if God would render himself visible to men, he would choose light for his body and truth for his soul.

—*Pythagoras (580 BC–500 BC)*

✦

It is one of the most beautiful compensations of life, that no man can sincerely try to help another without helping himself.

—*Ralph Waldo Emerson (1803–1882)*

✦

Is uniformity attainable? Millions of innocent men, women and children, since the introduction of Christianity, have been burnt, tortured, fined, imprisoned; yet we have not advanced an inch towards uniformity. What has been the effect of coercion? To make one half the world fools, and the other half hypocrites. To support roguery and error all over the earth.

—*Thomas Jefferson (1762–1826)*

Except our own thoughts, there is nothing absolutely in our power.

—*Rene Descartes (1596–1650)*

✦

Why not let people differ about their answers to the great mysteries of the Universe? Let each seek one's own way to the highest, to one's own sense of supreme loyalty in life, one's ideal of life. Let each philosophy, each world-view bring forth its truth and beauty to a larger perspective, that people may grow in vision, stature and dedication.

—*Algernon Black (1900–1995)*

✦

The best remedy for those who are afraid, lonely or unhappy is to go outside, somewhere where they can be quiet, alone with the heavens, nature and God. Because only then does one feel that all is as it should be and that God wishes to see people happy, amidst the simple beauty of nature.

—*Anne Frank (1929–1945)*

✦

In religion and politics people's beliefs and convictions are in almost every case gotten at second-hand, and without examination, from authorities who have not themselves examined the questions at issue but have taken them at second-hand from other non-examiners, whose opinions about them were not worth a brass farthing.

—*Mark Twain (1835–1910)*

The boundaries between life and death are at best shadowy and vague. Who shall say where one ends and where the other begins?

—Edgar Allan Poe (1809–1849)

✦

The man who says to me, "Believe as I do, or God will damn you," will presently say, "Believe as I do, or I shall assassinate you."

—Voltaire (1694–1778)

✦

It is my conviction that it is the intuitive, spiritual aspects of us humans—the inner voice—that gives us the 'knowing,' the peace, and the direction to go through the windstorms of life, not shattered but whole, joining in love and understanding.

—Elisabeth Kübler-Ross (1926–2004)

✦

It is better to have no opinion of God at all than such as one as is unworthy of him; for the one is only unbelief—the other is contempt.

—Plutarch (46 AD–119 AD)

We must not, like the frog in the well who imagines that the universe ends with the wall surrounding his well, think that our religion alone represents the whole Truth and all others are false.

—*Mahatma Gandhi (1869–1948)*

✦

The Christian churches were offered two things: the spirit of Jesus and the idiotic morality of Paul, and they rejected the higher inspiration. Following Paul, we have turned the goodness of love into a fiend and degraded the crowning impulse of our being into a capital sin.

—*Frank Harris (1856–1931)*

✦

The truly religious man does not embrace a religion; and he who embraces one has no religion.

—*Kahlil Gibran (1883–1931)*

✦

What do I believe? As an American I believe in generosity, in liberty, in the rights of man. These are social and political faiths that are part of me, as they are, I suppose, part of all of us. Such beliefs are easy to express. But part of me too is my relation to all life, my religion. And this is not so easy to talk about. Religious experience is highly intimate and, for me, ready words are not at hand.

—*Adlai E. Stevenson (1900–1965)*

At least two thirds of our miseries spring from human stupidity, human malice and those great motivators and justifiers of malice and stupidity, idealism, dogmatism and proselytizing zeal on behalf of religious or political idols.

—Aldous Huxley (1894–1963)

✦

Doing good to others is not a duty, it is a joy, for it increases our own health and happiness.

—Zoroaster (628 BC–551 BC)

✦

If we look back into history for the character of the present sects in Christianity, we shall find few that have not in their turns been persecutors, and complainers of persecution. The primitive Christians thought persecution extremely wrong in the Pagans, but practiced it on one another. The first Protestants of the Church of England blamed persecution in the Romish Church, but practiced it upon the Puritans. These found it wrong in the bishops, but fell into the same practice themselves both here (England) and in New England.

—Benjamin Franklin (1706–1790)

✦

God is a comedian playing to an audience too afraid to laugh.

—Voltaire (1694–1778)

A man's ethical behavior should be based effectually on sympathy, education, and social ties; no religious basis is necessary. Man would indeed be in a poor way if he had to be restrained by fear of punishment and hope of reward after death.

—Albert Einstein (1879–1955)

✦

We are in fact convinced that if we are ever to have pure knowledge of anything, we must get rid of the body and contemplate things by themselves with the soul by itself. It seems, to judge from the argument, that the wisdom which we desire and upon which we profess to have set our hearts will be attainable only when we are dead and not in our lifetime.

—Socrates (470 BC–399 BC)

✦

Is it so bad, then, to be misunderstood? Pythagoras was misunderstood, and Socrates, and Jesus, and Luther, and Copernicus, and Galileo, and Newton, and every pure and wise spirit that ever took flesh. To be great is to be misunderstood.

—Ralph Waldo Emerson (1803–1882)

✦

Real success is not on the stage, but off the stage as a human being, and how you get along with your fellow man.

—Sammy Davis, Jr. (1925–1990)

When any government, or church for that matter, undertakes to say to it's subjects, this you may not read, this you must not see, this you are forbidden to know, the end result is tyranny and oppression, no matter how holy the motive.

—*Robert Heinlein (1907–1988)*

✦

Religion and science both profess peace (and the sincerity of the professors is not being doubted), but each always turns out to have a dominant part in any war that is going or contemplated.

—*Howard Nemerov (1920–1991)*

✦

The common dogma [of fundamentalists] is fear of modern knowledge, inability to cope with the fast change in a scientific-technological society, and the real breakdown in apparent moral order in recent years. That is why hate is the major fuel, fear is the cement of the movement, and superstitious ignorance is the best defense against the dangerous new knowledge. When you bring up arguments that cast serious doubts on their cherished beliefs you are not simply making a rhetorical point, you are threatening their whole Universe and their immortality. That provokes anger and quite frequently violence. Unfortunately you cannot reason with them and you even risk violence in confronting them.

—*Author Unknown*

Religion is comparable to a childhood neurosis.

—Sigmund Freud (1856–1939)

✦

I contemplate with sovereign reverence the act of the whole American people which declared that their legislature should 'make no law respecting an establishment of religion, or prohibiting the free exercise thereof,' thus building a wall of separation between church and state.

—Thomas Jefferson (1762–1826)

✦

All religions show the same disparity between belief and practice, and each is safe till it tries to exclude the rest. Test each sect by its best or its worst as you will, by its high-water mark of virtue or its low-water mark of vice. But falsehood begins when you measure the ebb of any other religion against the flood-tide of your own. There is a noble and a base side to every history.

—Thomas Wentworth Higginson (1823–1911)

✦

To become a popular religion, it is only necessary for a superstition to enslave a philosophy.

—William Inge (1860–1954)

If a man does not keep pace with his companions, perhaps it is because he hears a different drummer. Let him step to the music which he hears, however measured or far away.

—*Henry David Thoreau (1817–1862)*

✦

Whenever we read the obscene stories, the voluptuous debaucheries, the cruel and torturous executions, the unrelenting vindictiveness, with which more than half the Bible is filled, it would be more consistent that we called it the word of a demon than the Word of God. It is a history of wickedness that has served to corrupt and brutalize mankind.

—*Thomas Paine (1737–1809)*

✦

Always observe how ephemeral and worthless human things are. Pass then through this little space of time conformably to nature, and end thy journey in content, just as an olive falls off when it is ripe, blessing nature who produced it, and thanking the tree on which it grew.

—*Marcus Aurelius (121 AD–180 AD)*

✦

Every day people are straying away from the church and going back to God.

—*Lenny Bruce (1925–1966)*

But theological change happens though selective quoting. Every religious person does it: You quote those verses that resonate with your own religious insights and ignore or reinterpret those that undermine your certainties. Selective quoting isn't just legitimate, but essential: Religions evolve through shifts in selective quoting.

—*Yossi Klein Halevi*

✦

What, then, does Jesus mean to me? To me He was one of the greatest teachers humanity has ever had. To His believers He was God's only begotten Son. Could the fact that I do or do not accept this belief make Jesus have any more or less influence in my life? Is all the grandeur of His teaching and of His doctrine to be forbidden to me? I cannot believe so. To me it implies a spiritual birth. My interpretation, in other words, is that in Jesus' own life is the key of His nearness to God; that He expressed, as no other could, the spirit and will of God. It is in this sense that I see Him and recognize Him as the Son of God.

—*Mahatma Gandhi (1869–1948)*

✦

The most preposterous notion that H. sapiens has ever dreamed up is that the Lord God of Creation, Shaper and Ruler of all the Universes, wants the saccharine adoration of His creatures, can be swayed by their prayers, and becomes petulant if He does not receive this flattery. Yet this absurd fantasy, without a shred of evidence to bolster it, pays all the expenses of the oldest, largest, and least productive industry in all history.

—*Robert Heinlein (1907–1988)*

That old law about 'an eye for an eye' leaves everybody blind. The time is always right to do the right thing.

—*Martin Luther King Jr. (1929–1968)*

✦

If you cannot find peace within yourself, you will never find it anywhere else.

—*Marvin Gaye (1939–1984)*

✦

Among the sayings and discourses imputed to him by his biographers, I find many passages of fine imagination, correct morality, and of the most lovely benevolence; and others, again, of so much ignorance, so much absurdity, so much untruth, charlatanism and imposture, as to pronounce it impossible that such contradictions should have proceeded from the same being. I separate, therefore, the gold from the dross; restore him to the former, and leave the latter to the stupidity of some, the roguery of others of his disciples. Of this band of dupes and imposters, Paul was the great Coryphaeus, and the first corruptor of the doctrines of Jesus.

—*Thomas Jefferson (1762–1826)*

✦

The more I study religions the more I am convinced that man never worshipped anything but himself.

—*Sir Richard Francis Burton (1821–1890)*

I learned this, at least, by my experiment: that if one advances confidently in the direction of his dreams, and endeavours to live the life which he has imagined, he will meet with a success unexpected in common hours. He will put some things behind, will pass an invisible boundary; new, universal, and more liberal laws will begin to establish themselves around and within him; or the old laws be expanded, and interpreted in his favour in a more liberal sense, and he will live with the license of a higher order of beings. In proportion as he simplifies his life, the laws of the universe will appear less complex, and solitude will not be solitude, nor poverty poverty, nor weakness weakness. If you have built castles in the air, your work need not be lost; that is where they should be. Now put the foundations under them.

—Henry David Thoreau (1817–1862)

✦

And who can doubt that it will lead to the worst disorders when minds created free by God are compelled to submit slavishly to an outside will? When we are told to deny our senses and subject them to the whim of others? When people devoid of whatsoever competence are made judges over experts and are granted authority to treat them as they please? These are the novelties which are apt to bring about the ruin of commonwealths and the subversion of the state.

—Galileo Galilei (1564–1642)

✦

All religions must be tolerated…for…every man must get to heaven in his own way.

—Epictetus (55 AD–135 AD)

True religion is real living; living with all one's soul, with all one's goodness and righteousness.

—*Albert Einstein (1879–1955)*

✦

Everybody prays whether [you think] of it as praying or not. The odd silence you fall into when something very beautiful is happening or something very good or very bad. The ah-h-h-h! that sometimes floats up out of you as out of a Fourth of July crowd when the sky-rocket bursts over the water. The stammer of pain at somebody else's pain. The stammer of joy at somebody else's joy. Whatever words or sounds you use for sighing with over your own life. These are all prayers in their way. These are all spoken not just to yourself but to something even more familiar than yourself and even more strange than the world.

—*Frederick Buechner (1926–)*

✦

Today the god hypothesis has ceased to be scientifically tenable…and its abandonment often brings a deep sense of relief. Many people assert that this abandonment of the god hypothesis means the abandonment of all religion and all moral sanctions. This is simply not true. But it does mean, once our relief at jettisoning an outdated piece of ideological furniture is over, that we must construct some thing to take its place.

—*Sir Julian Huxley (1887–1975)*

If I were personally to define religion I would say that it is a bandage that man has invented to protect a soul made bloody by circumstance.

—Theodore Dreiser (1871–1945)

✦

All souls were created in the beginning and are finding their way back to whence they came.

—Edgar Cayce (1877–1945)

✦

I believe in God, but not as one thing, not as an old man in the sky. I believe that what people call God is something in all of us. I believe that what Jesus and Mohammed and Buddha and all the rest said was right. It's just that the translations have gone wrong.

—John Lennon (1940–1980)

✦

The great enemy of the truth is very often not the lie—deliberate, contrived and dishonest—but the myth—persistent, persuasive and unrealistic.

—John F. Kennedy (1917–1963)

Religion is the masterpiece of the art of animal training, for it trains
people as to how they shall think.

—*Arthur Schopenhauer (1788–1860)*

✦

Humanity has in the course of time had to endure from the hands of
science two great outrages upon its naive self-love. The first was when
it realized that our earth was not the center of the universe, but only a
speck in a world-system of a magnitude hardly conceivable…The
second was when biological research robbed man of his particular
privilege of having been specially created, and relegated him to a
descent from the animal world.

—*Sigmund Freud (1856–1939)*

✦

We ought to do good to others as simply as a horse runs, or a bee
makes honey, or a vine bears grapes season after season without
thinking of the grapes it has borne.

—*Marcus Aurelius (121 AD–180 AD)*

✦

There were honest people long before there were Christians and there
are, God be praised, still honest people where there are no Christians.
It could therefore easily be possible that people are Christians because
true Christianity corresponds to what they would have been even if
Christianity did not exist.

—*Georg Christoph Lichtenberg (1742–1799)*

On the dogmas of religion, as distinguished from moral principles, all mankind, from the beginning of the world to this day, have been quarreling, fighting, burning and torturing one another, for abstractions unintelligible to themselves and to all others, and absolutely beyond the comprehension of the human mind.

—*Thomas Jefferson (1762–1826)*

✦

Nothing physical which sense-experience sets before our eyes, or which necessary demonstrations prove to us, ought to be called into question (much less condemned) upon the testimony of biblical passages.

—*Galileo Galilei (1564–1642)*

✦

All religion, my friend, is simply evolved out of fraud, fear, greed, imagination, and poetry.

—*Edgar Allan Poe (1809–1849)*

✦

I believe in the fundamental Truth of all the great religions of the world. I believe that they are all God given. I came to the conclusion long ago…that all religions were true and also that all had some error in them.

—*Mahatma Gandhi (1869–1948)*

All schools, all colleges, have two great functions: to confer, and to conceal, valuable knowledge. The theological knowledge which they conceal cannot justly be regarded as less valuable than that which they reveal. That is, when a man is buying a basket of strawberries it can profit him to know that the bottom half of it is rotten.

—*Mark Twain (1835–1910)*

✦

The religion that is afraid of science dishonors God and commits suicide.

—*Ralph Waldo Emerson (1803–1882)*

✦

Independence is my happiness, and I view things as they are, without regard to place or person; my country is the world, and my religion is to do good.

—*Thomas Paine (1737–1809)*

✦

Christianity might be a good thing if anyone ever tried it.

—*George Bernard Shaw (1856–1950)*

The purpose of separation of church and state is to keep forever from these shores the ceaseless strife that has soaked the soil of Europe with blood for centuries.

—*James Madison (1751–1836)*

✦

The opposite of the religious fanatic is not the fanatical atheist but the gentle cynic who cares not whether there is a god or not.

—*Eric Hoffer (1902–1983)*

✦

People who want to share their religious views with you almost never want you to share your's with them.

—*Dave Barry (1947–)*

✦

Men create gods after their own image, not only with regard to their form but with regard to their mode of life.

—*Aristotle (384 BC–322 BC)*

Thinking you know when in fact you don't is a fatal mistake, to which we are all prone.

—*Bertrand Russell (1872–1970)*

✦

A religion old or new, that stressed the magnificence of the universe as revealed by modern science, might be able to draw forth reserves of reverence and awe hardly tapped by the conventional faiths. Sooner or later, such a religion will emerge.

—*Dr. Carl Sagan (1934–1996)*

✦

There is not any thing, which has contributed so much to delude mankind in religious matters, as mistaken apprehensions concerning supernatural inspiration or revelation; not considering that all true religion originates from reason, and can not otherwise be understood, but by the exercise and improvement of it.

—*Ethan Allen (1738–1789)*

✦

To know that we know what we know, and to know that we do not know what we do not know, that is true knowledge.

—*Copernicus (1473–1543)*

Myths which are believed in tend to become true.

—*George Orwell (1903–1950)*

✦

The happiness of your life depends upon the quality of your thoughts: therefore, guard accordingly, and take care that you entertain no notions unsuitable to virtue and reasonable nature.

—*Marcus Aurelius (121 AD–180 AD)*

✦

And I have no doubt that every new example will succeed, as every past one has done, in showing that religion and Government will both exist in greater purity, the less they are mixed together.

—*James Madison (1751–1836)*

✦

All religions, arts and sciences are branches of the same tree. All these aspirations are directed toward ennobling man's life, lifting it from the sphere of mere physical existence and leading the individual towards freedom.

—*Albert Einstein (1879–1955)*

In the matter of religion, people eagerly fasten their eyes on the difference between their own creed and yours; whilst the charm of the study is in finding the agreements and identities in all the religions of humanity.

—Ralph Waldo Emerson (1803–1882)

✦

Ignorance is preferable to error, and he is less remote from the truth who believes nothing than he who believes what is wrong.

—Thomas Jefferson (1762–1826)

✦

Do not form views in the world through either knowledge, virtuous conduct, or religious observances; likewise, avoid thinking of oneself as being either superior, inferior, or equal to others. The wise let go of the "self" and being free of attachments they depend not on knowledge. Nor do they dispute opinions or settle into any view. For those who have no wishes for either extremes of becoming or non-becoming, here or in another existence, there is no settling into the views held by others. Nor do they form the least notion in regard to views seen, heard, or thought out. How could one influence those wise ones who do not grasp at any views.

—From the Sutta-nipata

I say quite deliberately that the Christian religion, as organized in its churches, has been and still is the principal enemy of moral progress in the world.

—*Bertrand Russell (1872–1970)*

✦

The purpose of separation of church and state is to keep forever from these shores the ceaseless strife that has soaked the soil of Europe with blood for centuries.

—*James Madison (1751–1836)*

✦

Do what's right for you, as long as it don't hurt no one.

—*Elvis Presley (1935–1977)*

✦

Waste no more time arguing about what a good man should be. Be one.

—*Marcus Aurelius (121 AD–180 AD)*

Religion is what keeps the poor man from murdering the rich.

—*Napoleon Bonaparte (1769–1821)*

✦

Heresy is only another word for freedom of thought.

—*Graham Greene (1904–1991)*

✦

The devil can cite Scripture for his purpose.

— *William Shakespeare (1564–1616)*
From "The Merchant of Venice"

✦

Religion is love; in no case is it logic.

—*Beatrice Potter Webb (1858–1943)*

The Bible is a book that has been read more and examined less than any book that ever existed.

—*Thomas Paine (1737–1809)*

✦

We're here for a reason. I believe a bit of the reason is to throw little torches out to lead people through the dark.

—*Whoopi Goldberg (1955–)*

✦

He who begins by loving Christianity better than truth, will proceed by loving his own sect or church better than Christianity, and end in loving himself better than all.

—*Samuel Taylor Coleridge (1772–1834)*

✦

Be not simply good; be good for something.

—*Henry David Thoreau (1817–1862)*

In seeking truth you have to get both sides of a story.

—*Walter Cronkite (1916–)*

✦

Every man dies. Not every man really lives.

—*"William Wallace" in*
Braveheart

✦

What else is nature but God?

—*Seneca (3 BC–65 AD)*

✦

All Bibles are man-made.

—*Thomas Edison (1847–1931)*

Religion is the reaction of human nature to its search for God.

—Alfred North Whitehead (1861–1947)

✦

Conscience is God's presence in man.

—Emanuel Swedenborg (1688–1772)

✦

I don't pretend we have all the answers. But the questions are certainly worth thinking about.

—Arthur C. Clarke (1917–)

✦

To know that you know, and to know that you don't know–that is the real wisdom.

—Confucius (551 BC–479 BC)

Let the human mind loose. It must be loose. It will be loose.
Superstition and dogmatism cannot confine it

—*John Adams (1735–1826)*

◆

You grow to heaven. You don't go to heaven.

—*Edgar Cayce (1877–1945)*

◆

I believe in God, only I spell it Nature.

—*Frank Lloyd Wright (1867–1959)*

◆

To find yourself, think for yourself.

—*Socrates (470 BC–399 BC)*

All you need is love.

—John Lennon (1940–1980)

✦

God has no religion.

—Mahatma Gandhi (1869–1948)

Afterword

As I stated in the introduction, this book was not meant to be anti-religion (although many of the sources may seem to sound that way). The very fact that you are now reading these words demonstrates that you are an open-minded individual. And for that, I am very grateful. My brother recently asked me, "Mark, why don't you just write a book filled with your own thoughts about religion and spirituality, and maybe throw in a famous quote or two. After all, your words are equally as valid as their words." Well, the truth is, I could have written many of the words that appeared in this book, but I don't think they would have had the same impact.

Most organized religions seem to have one common flaw: they tend to put more importance on the *messenger* than they do on the *message*. It seems to me this is the major problem. Too much time spent on the symbols of the religion and not enough time spent living the simple message: "Love one another." Which simply means take care of one another…every single being on this planet. What is so difficult about that?

I really do believe religion has the capacity to be a very good thing. But unfortunately, as history (and the present) has demonstrated all too often, it equally has the capacity to be…not so good. That's why each of us needs to examine our own personal spirituality, our own personal "truths", and if some part of a particular religion doesn't sound logical or within reason to us…discard it, and not follow blindly simply because someone else (in my case, a TV preacher) says it is right to do so. Better yet, it might be easier to just contemplate the simple truth of the words on the last page of this book:

"God has no religion."

Glossary

This is a very brief glossary of the sources in this book. If you wish to research the validity of these quotes, a wealth of information can be found on the internet and at your local library.

A

John Adams (1735–1826): One of America's Founding Fathers and framers of the American Constitution. Second President of the United States.

Alan Alda (1936–): American actor. Best remembered for the role of Hawkeye Pierce on the television series *M*A*S*H*.

Ethan Allen (1738–1789): Farmer turned statesman from Connecticut. A soldier in the American Revolution and leader of the Green Mountain Boys.

Thea Alexander (1936–): American author of the wonderful novel *2150 AD*.

Alexander the Great (356 BC–323 BC): One of the greatest generals in history. Became King of Macedon and conquered much of Asia.

Susan B. Anthony (1820–1906): A leader in the women's rights movement of the nineteenth century. Quaker, teacher, temperance and abolition organizer.

Aristotle (384 BC–322 BC): Ancient Greek philosopher, physician, and scientist. He studied under Plato and turored Alexander the Great.

Isaac Asimov (1920–1992): Russian-born American science-fiction writer. Books include *The Naked Sun* and *The Gods Themselves.*

Marcus Aurelius (121 AD–180 AD): Roman emperor. One of the great intellectual rulers in Western Civilization. Author of *Meditations* expressing his Stoic philosophy.

B

Dave Barry (1947–): American writer and humorist.

Pierre Bayle (1647–1706): French philosopher, writer, and critic. Became a professor of philosophy at the Calvinist academy of Sedan.

Algernon Black (1900–1995): Was a member of the Board of Leaders of the New York Society for Ethical Culture, and head of the Ethics Department in the Ethical Culture Schools.

Henry Bolingbroke (1678-1751): Became King Henry IV of England. Son of John of Gaunt and grandson of Edward III. He founded the Lancastrian dynasty.

Napoleon Bonaparte (1769–1821): French general. Became Emperor of France.

Phyllis Bottome (1884–1963): English novelist and lecturer. Novels include *The Mortal Storm*, and *London Pride.*

Lenny Bruce (1925–1966): American stand-up comedian and satirist.

Jean de la Bruyère (1645–1696): French moralist and teacher.

Pearl S. Buck (1892–1973): Popular American author, humanitarian, crusader for women's rights, and philanthropist. Awarded the Nobel Prize for Literature in 1938.

Frederick Buechner (1926–): American author. Novels include *A Long Day's Dying* and *The Season's Difference.*

Sophy Burnham (1936–): Award-winning American author. Books include *The Art Crowd* and *A Book of Angels.*

Sir Richard Francis Burton (1821–1890): English explorer, linguist, author, and soldier. Translated the *Arabian Nights* and the *Kama Sutra* into English.

C

Joseph Campbell (1904–1987): American writer on mythology and comparative religion. Books include *The Masks of God: Primitive Mythology* and *The Hero with a Thousand Faces.*

George Washington Carver (1864–1943): American inventor, born of slave parents in Missouri. Developed crop-rotation methods for conserving nutrients in soil. Developed 325 different uses for peanuts.

Catullus (84 BC–54 BC): Roman poet.

Edgar Cayce (1877–1945): American psychic. Known as "the sleeping prophet" because he would close his eyes and appear to go into a trance state when he did his readings.

Pierre Teilhard de Chardin (1881–1955): French Jesuit, paleontologist, writer, and philosopher. Spent much of his life trying to integrate religious experience with natural science.

Chief Seattle (1786–1866): Became chief of the Suquamish and Duwamish tribes. Widely respected among the Indians.

Deepak Chopra (1947–): Best-selling author. Books include *The Seven Spiritual Laws of Success* and *Ageless Body, Timeless Mind.*

Arthur C. Clarke (1917–): English-born science-fiction writer. Books include *2001: A Space Odyssey* and *Rendezvous with Rama.*

William Cobbett (1763–1835): English journalist and publisher of the *Political Register,* the main newspaper read by the working class.

Samuel Taylor Coleridge (1772–1834): English poet, critic and philosopher. A leader of the romantic movement. Poems include *Kubla Khan* and *Rime of the Ancient Mariner.*

Confucius (551 BC–479 BC): Chinese philosopher and teacher.

Copernicus (1473–1543): Polish astronomer. Born Mikolaj Kopernik. Proponent of the Heliocentric theory that the Sun, and not the Earth, is at rest in the center of the Universe.

Norman Cousins (1912–1990): American writer and long-time editor of *Saturday Review.* Wrote *Anatomy of an Illness* describing how watching Marx Brothers movies helped him recover from a life-threatening disease.

Walter Cronkite (1916–): Long time news anchorman for the American television network CBS. Once considered the most trusted man in America.

D

Dalai Lama (1935–): Tenzin Gyatso. The spiritual and temporal leader of the Tibetan people. He is the fourteenth Dalai Lama and recipient of the Nobel Peace Prize in 1989.

Clarence Darrow (1857–1938): American lawyer. Most famous for his case defending John Scopes, a teacher accused of teaching the evolutionary origin of man rather than the doctrine of divine creation. The play *Inherit the Wind* is based on this trial.

Charles Darwin (1809–1882): English naturalist. Author of the theory of evolution by natural selection.

Sammy Davis, Jr. (1925–1990): Great American singer, actor, and dancer. Known throughout much of his career as "the world's greatest living entertainer."

Rene Descartes (1596–1650): French mathematician, scientist, and philosopher. Most famous quote: "I think, therefore I am."

Benjamin Disraeli (1804–1881): English statesman. Became Prime Minister in 1868. Writer of the political novels *Coningsby* and *Sybil.*

Theodore Dreiser (1871–1945): American writer. Books include *The Financier* and *An American Tragedy.* Considered by many as the leader of Naturalism in American writing.

Dr. Wayne W. Dyer (1940–): American self-help author and motivational speaker. Books include *The Power of Intention* and *Your Erroneous Zones.*

E

Thomas Edison (1847–1931): One of the greatest and most productive inventors of all time. He was awarded over 1,300 patents during his lifetime.

Albert Einstein (1879–1955): German-born physicist. Famous for his Theory of Relativity. He received the Nobel Prize in Physics in 1921. For many, his name is synonymous with the word "genius".

Dwight D. Eisenhower (1890–1969): Commanding General in Europe during World War II. Became the thirty-fourth President of the United States.

Ralph Waldo Emerson (1803–1882): American essayist, poet, and philosopher. Best known for his essay *Self-Reliance*. Mentor and friend of Henry David Thoreau.

Epictetus (55 AD–135 AD): Greek philosopher, associated with the Stoics. He believed in the brotherhood of man.

F

Anatole France (1844–1924): French novelist and storyteller. Received the Nobel Prize in Literature in 1921.

Anne Frank (1929–1945): A German-Jewish teenager. She and her family went into hiding during the Holocaust in World War II. Anne died in a concentration camp at fifteen years of age.

Her diary was found, and is now one of the most widely read books in the world.

Benjamin Franklin (1706–1790): American printer, librarian, inventor, and statesman. One of America's Founding Fathers. Famous for his "kite-flying experiment" with electricity.

Sigmund Freud (1856–1939): Austrian physiologist, medical doctor, psychologist, and father of psychoanalysis. One of the most authoritative thinkers of the twentieth century.

G

Galileo Galilei (1564–1642): Italian astronomer and physicist. Pioneered the "experimental scientific method". His support of the Heliocentric (sun-centered) theory of the universe got him in trouble with the Roman Catholic Church, and the Inquisition convicted him of heresy.

Mahatma Gandhi (1869–1948): Mohandas K. Gandhi emerged as a national leader during India's fight for independence from Britain. Remembered for his practice of simplicity and principles of non-violence. He was given the title of 'Mahatma' or 'Great Soul'.

Greta Garbo (1905–1990): Swedish-born film star of the early twentieth century.

Siddhartha Gautama (563–483 BC): The Buddha (Enlightened One). Founder of Buddhism.

Marvin Gaye (1939–1984): American singer and songwriter.

Kahlil Gibran (1883–1931): Lebanese-American author. Famous for his book *The Prophet*.

Johann Wolfgang von Goethe (1749–1832): German writer and scientist. Known for his great dramatic poem *Faust*.

Vincent van Gogh (1853–1890): Famous Dutch artist.

Whoopi Goldberg (1955–): American actress and stand-up comedian.

Ulysses S. Grant (1822–1885): Union General during the Civil War. Became the eighteenth President of the United States.

Graham Greene (1904–1991): English writer. Books include *The Third Man* and *Loser Takes All.*

H

Lord Hailsham (1872–1950): British lawyer and politician.

Yossi Klein Halevi: Israeli journalist for the *Jerusalem Post* and the *New Republic.*

Thich Nhat Hanh (1926–): Vietnamese writer. Also a Buddhist monk and founder of Van Hanh Buddhist University. He was nominated by Dr. Martin Luther King, Jr. for the Nobel Peace Prize.

Frank Harris (1856–1931): English author and editor. He wrote the scandalous *My Life and Loves.*

George Harrison (1943–2001): English singer, songwriter, and guitarist. Best known as a member of the rock band *The Beatles.*

Robert Heinlein (1907–1988): Called "the Dean of science-fiction writers". Books include *Stranger in a Strange Land* and *Starship Troopers.*

Thomas Wentworth Higginson (1823–1911): American author, Unitarian minister, and a leader in the abolitionist movement.

Eric Hoffer (1902–1983): American writer and social philosopher. A recipient of the Presidential Medal of Freedom. Books include *The True Believer.*

Elbert Hubbard (1856–1915): American author and publisher. He edited the inspirational *Philistine* magazine.

L. Ron Hubbard (1911–1986): American author and founder of the Church of Scientology. He wrote *Dianetics: The Modern Science of Mental Health.*

David Hume (1711–1776): Scottish philosopher and historian.

Aldous Huxley (1894–1963): English author. Most famous for his book *Brave New World.*

Sir Julian Huxley (1887–1975): Brother of Aldous Huxley. English biologist and writer. His writings include *Animal Biology* and *The Living Thoughts of Darwin.*

I

William Inge (1860–1954): American playwright. Wrote *Come Back, Little Sheba* and *Bus Stop.*

J

Thomas Jefferson (1762–1826): One of America's Founding Fathers. Author of the Declaration of Independence. Became the third President of the United States.

Flavius Josephus (37 AD–100 AD): Jewish historian and soldier.

Carl Jung (1875–1961): Swiss psychiatrist and founder of analytical psychology.

K

Immanuel Kant (1724–1804): German metaphysician. His writings include *Critique of Pure Reason* and *Critique of Practical Reason.*

Helen Keller (1880–1968): American author and lecturer. Blind and deaf from an undiagnosed illness at the age of two. Her books include *The Story of my Life* and *The Open Door.*

John F. Kennedy (1917–1963): Thirty-fifth President of the United States. He received the Pulitzer Prize for his book *Profiles in Courage.* Assassinated by Lee Harvey Oswald (and possibly someone else).

Dr. Martin Luther King, Jr. (1929–1968): American clergyman and civil rights leader. Awarded the Nobel Peace Prize in 1964. He wrote *Stride Toward Freedom* and *Why We Can't Wait.*

Jiddu Krishnamurti (1895–1986): Indian writer and lecturer whose message centered on the need for maximum self-awareness. Writings include *Life in Freedom* and *Think on These Things.*

Louis Kronenberger (1904–1980): American writer and drama critic.

Elisabeth Kübler-Ross (1926–2004): American psychiatrist, born in Switzerland. Most famous for her book *On death and Dying.*

L

Lao-tzu (Born 600 BC): Chinese philosopher. Credited as the founder of Taoism.

D.H. Lawrence (1885–1930): English author. Writings include *The Rainbow* and the controversial *Lady Chatterley's Lover*.

John Lennon (1940–1980): English singer and songwriter. Best remembered as a member of the rock band *The Beatles*.

Andrew Lias: American athiest, rationalist, and "neo-platonist".

Georg Christoph Lichtenberg (1742–1799): German physicist and satirist. Specialized in electricity.

Abraham Lincoln (1809–1865): Sixteenth President of the United States. Assassinated by John Wilkes Booth.

M

Shirley MacLaine (1934–): American actress, dancer, singer, and author. Her books include *Out on a Limb* and *Going Within*.

James Madison (1751–1836): One of America's Founding Fathers. Became the fourth President of the United States.

Maimonides (1135–1204): Jewish scholar, physician, and philosopher. Also known as Moses ben Maimon. The most influential Jewish thinker of the Middle Ages.

W. Somerset Maugham (1874–1965): English writer. Novels include *Of Human Bondage* and *The Razor's Edge*.

Thomas Merton (1915–1968): American religious writer and poet. Works include *Seeds of Contemplation* and *The Silent Life.*

Michelangelo (1475–1564): Italian sculptor, painter, architect, and poet. Paintings include *The Last Judgement* and the ceiling of the Sistine Chapel.

Harvey Milk (1930–1978): American politician and gay rights activist. He was assassinated, along with San Francisco Mayor George Moscone, by former city supervisor Dan White.

Marilyn Monroe (1926–1962): Famous American movie star.

N

Howard Nemerov (1920–1991): American poet, novelist, and critic. Works include *The Image and the Law* and *Inside the Onion.*

Florence Nightingale (1820–1910): English nurse. The founder of modern nursing. Her life was dedicated to the care of the sick and war wounded.

Anais Nin (1903–1977): American writer, born in Paris. Daughter of the Spanish composer Joaquin Nin. Novels include *Winter of Artifice* and *A Spy in the House of Love.*

Richard M. Nixon (1913–1994): Thirty-seventh President of the United States. As a result of the Watergate scandal, he became the first President to resign the office.

Mirza Hoseyn Ali Nuri (1817-1892): Also known as Baha'u'llah, founder of the Baha'i faith. Baha'ists believe in the unity of all religions, in universal education, in world peace, and in the equality of men and women.

O

George Orwell (1903–1950): English novelist and essayist. Known for his satirical and frighteningly political novels. Novels include *Nineteen Eighty-Four* and *Coming Up for Air.*

Ovid (43 BC–17 AD): Latin poet. Famous in his early life, then, for no known reason, he was exiled to Tomis, a Black Sea outpost, where he later died.

P

Thomas Paine (1737–1809): American writer and political theorist. He wrote the pamphlet *Common Sense* arguing that the American colonies had outgrown the need for British domination.

Blaise Pascal (1623–1662): French scientist and religious philosopher.

Norman Vincent Peale (1898–1993): American minister and writer. One of the most influential clergymen of the twentieth century. Books include *The Power of Positive Thought* and *The Art of Living.*

Plato (428 BC–348 BC): Greek philosopher and writer. His teachings are among the most influential in the history of Western Civilization. He was a pupil and friend of Socrates.

Plutarch (46 AD–119 AD): Greek essayist and biographer. His work would later supply the material for many of William Shakespeare's plays including *Julius Ceasar* and *Antony and Cleopatra.*

Edgar Allan Poe (1809–1849): American poet, critic, and short-story writer. Works include *The Raven* and *The Murders in the Rue Morgue.*

Pope John Paul I (1912–1978): He was an Italian named Albino Luciani. Successor of Pope Paul VI. He died one month after becoming pope.

Karl Popper (1902–1994): Austrian philosopher. His works include *The Logic of Scientific Discovery* and *The Self and its Brain*.

Elvis Presley (1935–1977): Charismatic American singer. Dubbed the "King of Rock and Roll". A great influence on much of the music that followed.

Pythagoras (580 BC–500 BC): Greek philosopher. Founder of the Pythagorean School. The Pythagoreans are best known for their belief in the transmigration of souls (a form of reincarnation) and the theory that numbers constitute the nature of things.

R

Rembrandt (1606–1669): Famous Dutch painter and etcher. His works include *Three Trees* and *Christ Healing the Sick*.

Eleanor Roosevelt (1884–1962): American First Lady, humanitarian, and writer. Wife of President Franklin Roosevelt and neice of President Theodore Roosevelt.

Leo Rosten (1908–1997): Polish-born American author, teacher, and humorist. Books include *The Joys of Yiddish*.

Bertrand Russell (1872–1970): English philosopher and mathematician, lecturer, and social reformer. Books include *The Principles of Mathematics*.

S

Dr. Carl Sagan (1934–1996): American astronomer, writer, and scientist. Creator and host of the public television series *Cosmos*. He received a Pulitzer Prize in 1977 for *The Dragons of Eden*.

Arthur Schopenhauer (1788–1860): German philosopher. Works include *The World as Will and Representation* and *The Basis of Morality*.

Albert Schweitzer (1875–1965): Alsatian theologian, humanitarian, medical missionary, and musician. Recipient of the Nobel Peace Prize in 1952. Works include *The Quest of the Historical Jesus* and *The Mysticism of Paul the Apostle*.

Seneca (3 BC–65 AD): Roman philosopher, statesman, and dramatist. Plays attributed to Seneca include *Agamemnon* and *Medea*.

Anna Sewell (1820–1878): English author. Her only work, *Black Beauty*, became a children's classic.

Lord Anthony Ashley Cooper Shaftesbury III (1671-1713): English social reformer. During the Industrial Revolution he became a leading advocate of government action to eliminate injustices.

William Shakespeare (1564–1616): England's most famous dramatist and poet. He is considered the greatest playwright who ever lived.

George Bernard Shaw (1856–1950): Irish playwright and critic. He received the Nobel Prize in Literature in 1925. His works include *Man and Superman* and *Pygmalion*.

Percy Bysshe Shelley (1792–1822): English poet. His works include *Prometheus Unbound* and *Adonais*.

Socrates (470 BC–399 BC): Greek philosopher. A man who lived by his principles, even though they would ultimately cost him his life. He was a teacher and friend of Plato.

Gerry Spence (1929–): American trial lawyer. Author of *How to Argue and Win Every Time*.

Stendhal (1783–1842): French writer. Considered one of the great French novelists. Books include *De l'amour* and *Armance*.

Adlai E. Stevenson (1900–1965): American statesman. One-time Governor of Illinois. Ran for President, unsuccessfully, against Dwight D. Eisenhower. His works include *A Call to Greatness* and *Friends and Enemies*.

Robert Louis Stevenson (1850–1894): Scottish poet, novelist, and essayist. Popular works include *Kidnapped* and *Treasure Island*.

The Sutta-nipata: One of the oldest collections of Buddhist discourses. It presents a code of conduct and provides the basis for a system of moral philosophy.

Emanuel Swedenborg (1688–1772): Swedish religious teacher, scientist, and mystic. His works include *True Christian Religion* and *Divine Love and Wisdom*.

Jonathan Swift (1667–1745): English author and satirist.

Writer of the satirical masterpiece *Gulliver's Travels*.

T

Rabindranath Tagore (1861–1941): Indian author and guru. His works include *The Gardener* and *The Religion of Man*.

Henry David Thoreau (1817–1862): American author, naturalist, and trancendentalist. Friend of Ralph Waldo Emerson. Thoreau's works include *Walden* and *Civil Disobedience*.

Bishop Desmond Tutu (1931–): The first black Archbishop of Capetown, South Africa and head of the Anglican Church. He received the Nobel Peace Prize in 1984.

Mark Twain (1835–1910): American author and humorist. Born Samuel Clemens. Famous works include *The Adventures of Tom Sawyer* and *The Adventures of Huckleberry Finn*.

V

Voltaire (1694–1778): French philosopher and author. His philosophy was based on skepticism and rationalism. Notable works include *Candide* and *Dictionnaire Philosophique*.

W

William Wallace (1272?–1305): Scottish soldier and national hero. Featured in the movie *Braveheart*.

Neale Donald Walsch (1943–): American author of the best-selling *Conversations With God* series of books.

George Washington (1732–1799): One of America's Founding Fathers and the first President of the United States. He was Commander in Chief of the Continental army in the American Revolution.

Beatrice Potter Webb (1858–1943): English socialist economist and writer.

Alfred North Whitehead (1861–1947): English philosopher and mathematician. His works include *The Organisation of Thought* and *Religion in the Making*.

Walt Whitman (1819–1892): Considered by many to be the greatest of all American poets. His works include *Leaves of Grass* and *Drum-Taps*.

Oscar Wilde (1854–1900): Irish author noted for his brilliantly witty plays. Popular works include *The Importance of Being Earnest* and *A Woman of No Importance*.

William Wordsworth (1770–1850): English poet. A leader of the romantic movement in England. Works include *The Excursion* and *Memorials of a Tour of the Continent*.

Frank Lloyd Wright (1867–1959): Considered the greatest American architect.

Y

Yoda: Fictional character from the *Star Wars* series of films.

Lin Yutang (1895–1976): Chinese-American writer, editor, and translator. Works include *A Leaf in the Storm* and *My Country and My People*.

Z

Zoroaster (628 BC–551 BC): Religious teacher and prophet of ancient Persia. Founder of Zoroastrianism.